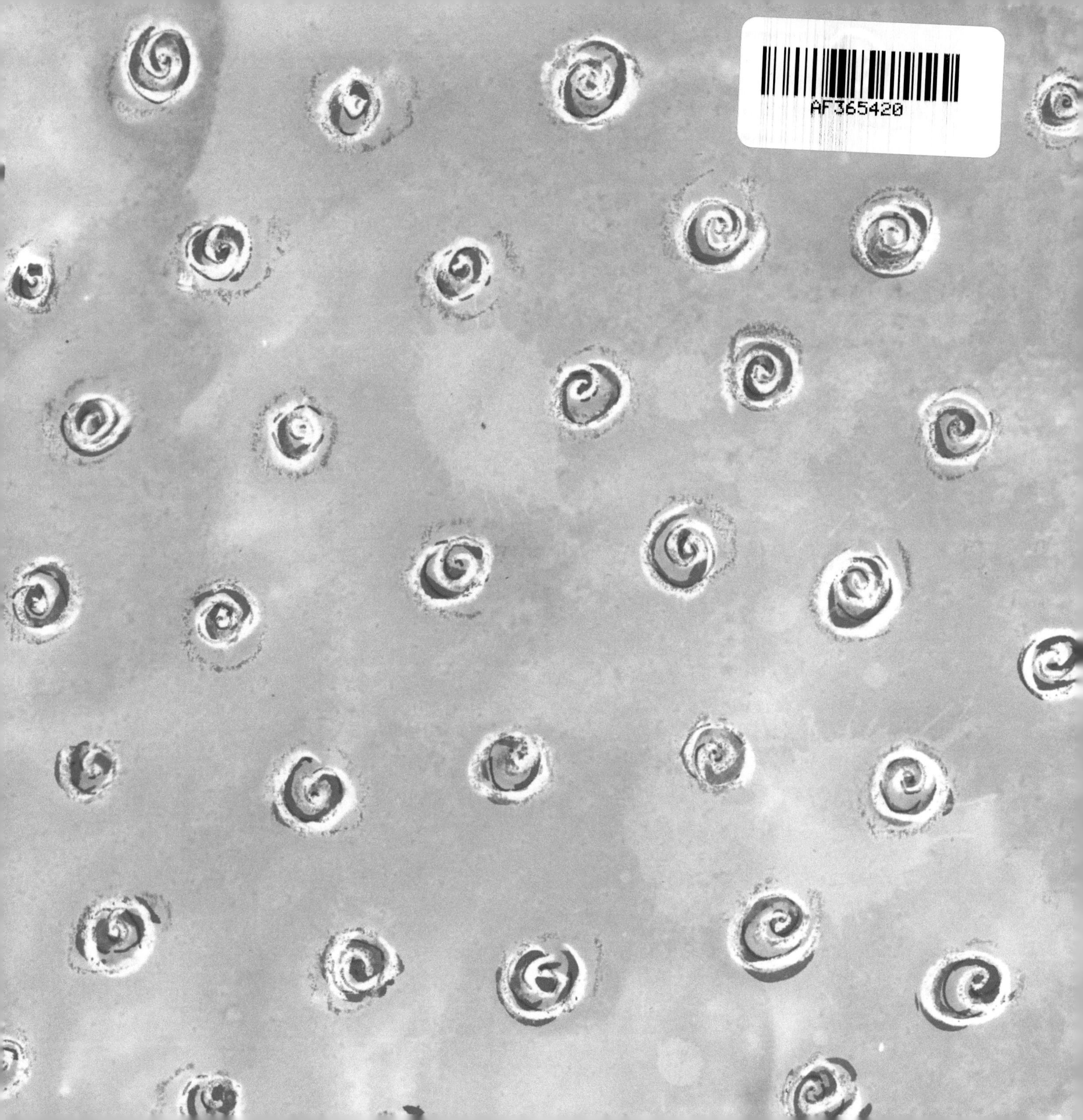
AF365420

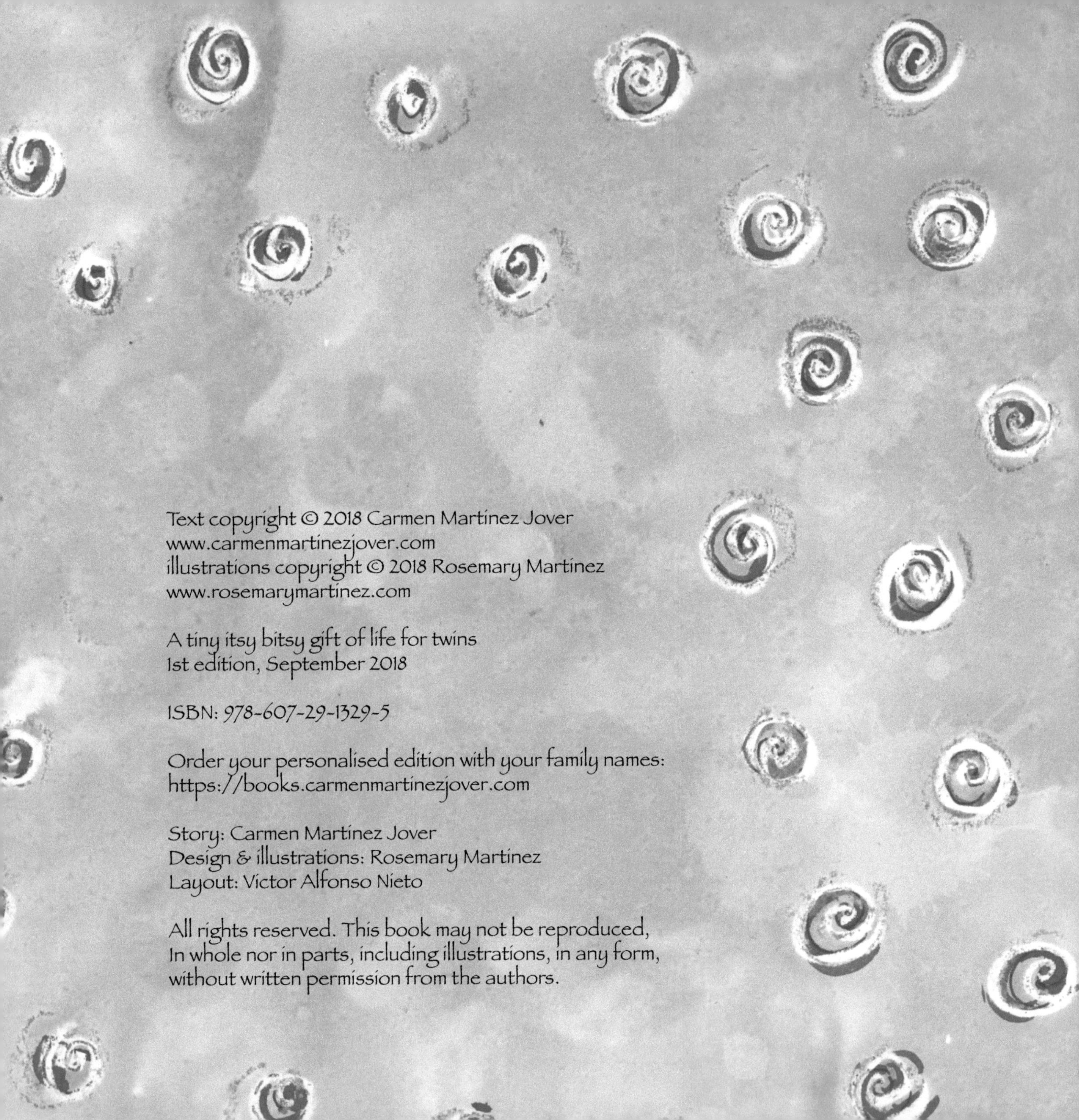

Text copyright © 2018 Carmen Martinez Jover
www.carmenmartinezjover.com
illustrations copyright © 2018 Rosemary Martinez
www.rosemarymartinez.com

A tiny itsy bitsy gift of life for twins
1st edition, September 2018

ISBN: 978-607-29-1329-5

Order your personalised edition with your family names:
https://books.carmenmartinezjover.com

Story: Carmen Martinez Jover
Design & illustrations: Rosemary Martinez
Layout: Victor Alfonso Nieto

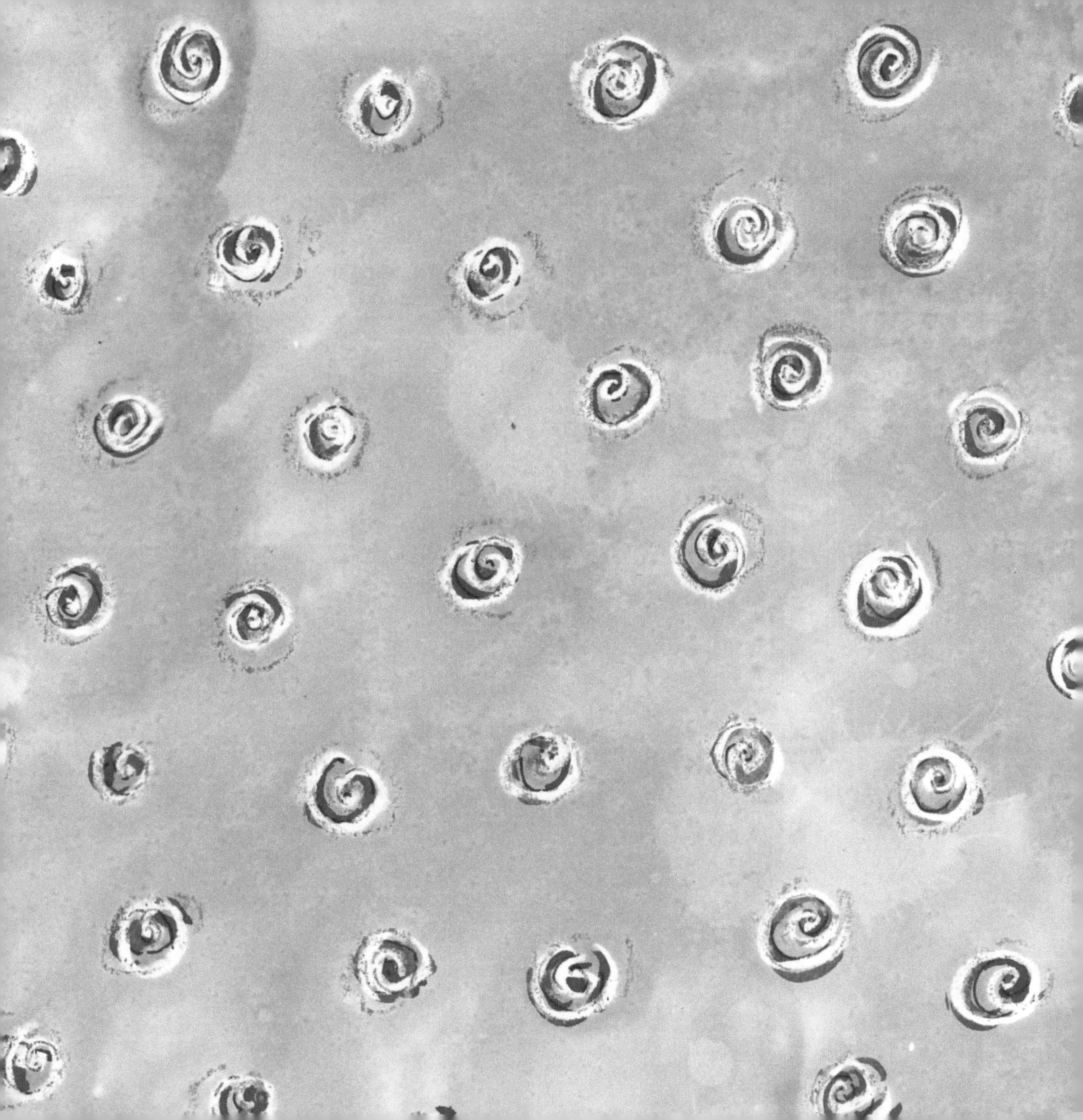

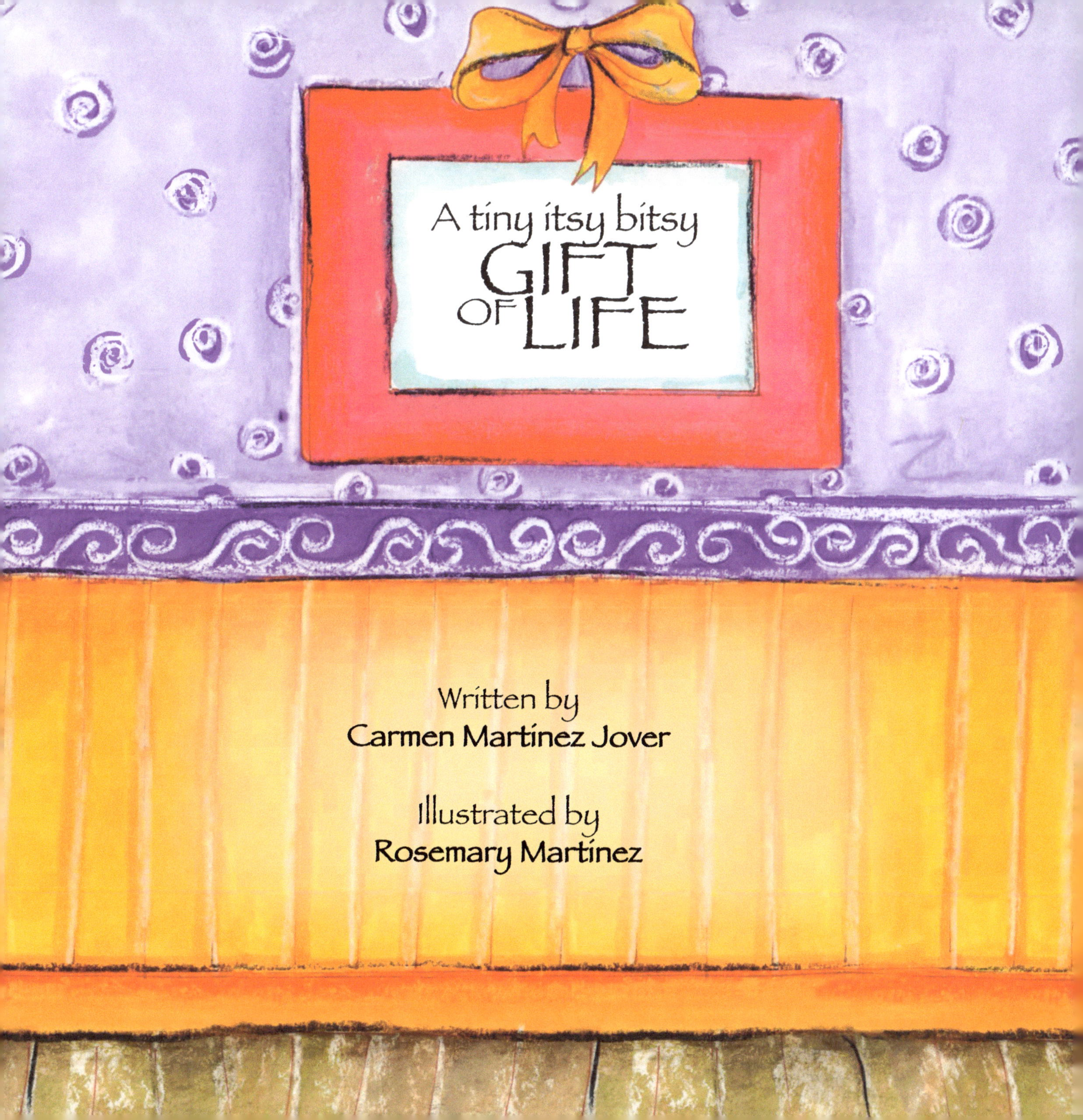

A tiny itsy bitsy GIFT OF LIFE

Written by
Carmen Martínez Jover

Illustrated by
Rosemary Martínez

I dedicate this book to my daughter
Nicole, for teaching me how, what
I was so afraid of sharing could be
so easy, and for teaching me how to
learn to listen to my heart.
Carmen

I dedicate this book to my parents
for teaching me that everything
is possible with love, and to
Joaquin, the love of my life,
for proving me that this is true.
Rosemary

Once upon a time there were
two rabbits: Comet and Pally.

They lived very happily
in their beautitul home.

They loved going to the park and
always saw lots of little bunnies everywhere,
but they didn't have theirs.

"I really want us to have our
own baby bunnies.
I can't wait until we become
a Mummy and Daddy,"
said Pally.

"Yes so do I!"
replied Comet.

10

"Let's see..." he said,
"to make a
baby bunny
we need
tiny itsy bitsy
seeds from you and
tiny itsy bitsy
seeds from me.

"Like this cookie:
two halves make one
or if we have two sets
of two halves, then we
have two cookies."

But, Spring went by...
and Summer went by...

and Autumn went by...

and Winter went by...

and Comet
and Pally had still
not become
a Mummy
and a Daddy.

13

The doctor told Pally that she had no more
itsy bitsy seeds left in her tummy
to make baby bunnies.

14

She felt very sad.

One special sunny
day, a lady rabbit
knocked on
the door.

They had never
seen her before.

"Hello Pally,
I have a gift
of life for you.

I have a lot of
tiny itsy bitsy seeds
and I want
to give you two.

These are the other
halves you need to have
your baby bunnies,"
she said.

Pally treasured these
tiny itsy bitsy gifts,
because she needed them
to have her baby bunnies.

And then Comet said,
"Look Pally, here I have
the other tiny itsy bitsy
halves we need.

These seeds together
will make our bunnies,
like the cookie, remember?"

"Now, lets put
my tiny itsy bitsy seeds
with your two
tiny itsy bitsy gifts
together in your tummy
so our baby bunnies
can grow,"
said Comet.

Soon Pally's
tummy started
to grow
and grow
and grow.

Comet would always
look after her.

Pally liked
eating lots of
delicious things so
that their baby bunnies,
that were growing in
her tummy, would grow
very healthy.

23

They started preparing their
baby bunnies bedroom.
It was the most beautiful and
loving room you have ever seen.

Finally, Pally and Comet
became a Mummy and Daddy!

The baby bunnies were born,
they were so beautiful
and they called them
Sam & Alex.

Sam & Alex grew...
and grew...
and grew...

and the lived happily
ever after as a family.

28

Carmen Martínez Jover is an fertility coach, author, artist and international lecturer. She is also the author of "I want to have a child, whatever it takes, an autobiography of her own infertility journey.
www.carmenmartinezjover.com

Rosemary Martínez
is an international award-winning
designer, and did the most amazing
illustrations which makes this story
so much fun to read with your kids.
www.rosemarymartinez.com

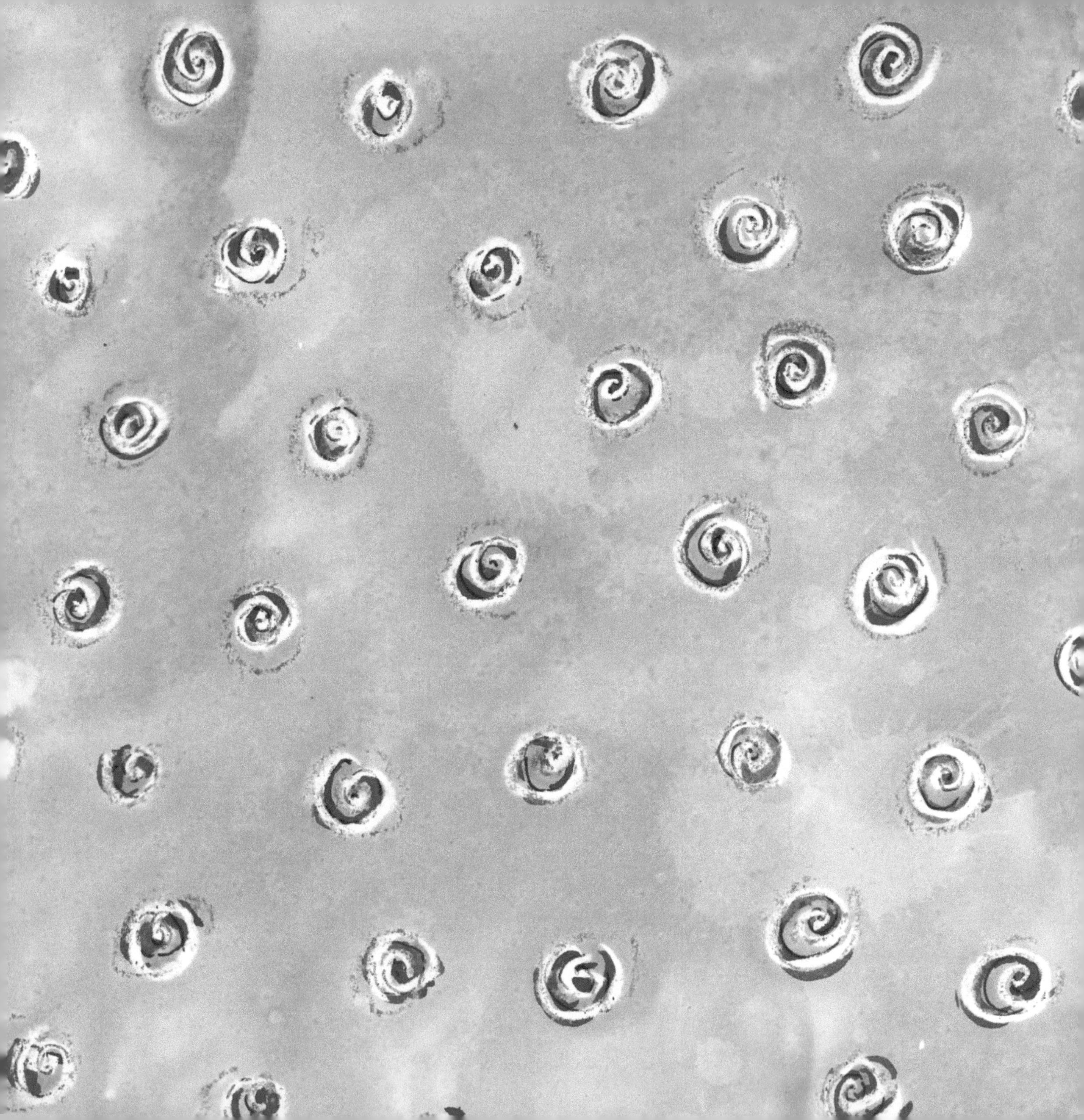

Be the **heroes** of **your** own story

Personalise your own story
with your own names

https://books.carmenmartinezjover.com

EGG DONATION

A tiny itsy bitsy gift of life, an egg donor story for girls, boys and twins. PERSONALISED

ADOPTION

Soul's Time to Reincarnate, an adoption story. PERSONALISED

SINGLE MUM BY CHOICE

Forever Together, a single mum by choice story for one child or twins. PERSONALISED

TWO DADS

The baby kangaroo treasure hunt, a gay parenting story for one child or twins. PERSONALISED

Other books by: Carmen Martinez Jover

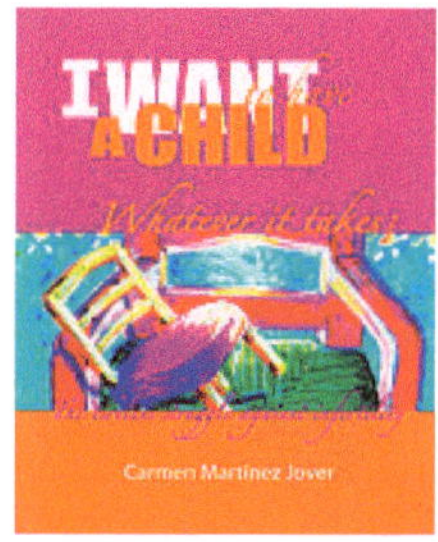

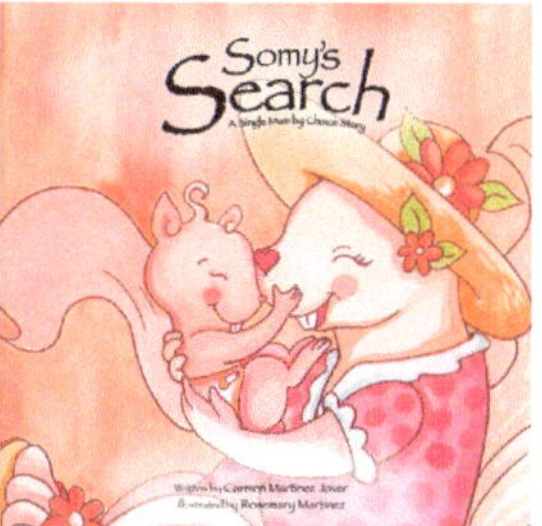

I want to have a child, whatever it takes!

Recipes of How Babies are Made

Somy's Search, a single mum by choice story

Available in:

www.amazon.com
www.carmenmartinezjover.com

English, Español, Français, Italiano, Português, Svenska, Русский, Nederlands